Soci   g
Workbook 2019

How to Leverage The Power of Facebook Advertising, Instagram Marketing, YouTube and SEO To Explode Your Business and Personal Brand

Written By

Adam Schaffner

Illustrations copyright © 2019 by Anna Marcia

Cover photography by Anna Marcia

First Edition: January 2019

ISBN - 109881407X

Produced by Adam Schaffner

Printed in the United States of America

Table of Contents

Preface 5

Chapter 1: Why Use Social Media and SEO For Your Brand in 2019 7

Chapter 2: Building a Personal Brand in 2019 13

Chapter 3: Building Your Core Brand Strategy: 5 Tips for Success 19

Chapter 4: Identifying Yourself & Creating Your Offer.. 25

Chapter 5: Instagram Marketing For Your Brand in 2019 31

Chapter 6:Instagram Stories 56

Chapter 7: Facebook................................66

Chapter 8: Facebook Advertising.............90

Chapter 9: Twitter 108

Chapter 10: Youtube............................... 140

Chapter 11: Social Media Strategy
Worksheet..164

Chapter 12: Search Engine Optimization
(SEO)..168

Chapter 13: SEO Worksheet.................... 177

Chapter 14: Tips and Tricks to Social Media
Marketing and SEO Success in 2019 181

Conclusion 187

Preface

Nowadays, it goes without saying that when someone starts their own business - whether it is selling products or services - they should create social media pages for it; and most people do. However, social media marketing is **often** seen by business owners as the simple process of creating a page and posting on it from time to time, when in reality it is **so much more** than that. It requires a well-established strategy and it needs to be monitored over time, just like any traditional marketing plan would.

Besides that, not having a website (or having one with a bad design and user experience) is a red flag for most consumers. Just think about what you do when you want to know more about a certain product, **brand or person.** You go straight to Google, **don't you?**

In this e-book, I will talk to you about **Social Media and SEO trends** and predictions for 2019, as well as tips and tricks that will help you achieve a better performance online when you promote your own personal brand. You will have blank space to take your notes so that, in the end, you will have everything you need to start and maintain a strategy for your brand on the Internet.

Chapter 1: Why Use Social Media and SEO For Your Brand in 2019

During the last few years, entrepreneurship and freelancing have been on the rise. So many people have been opening their own businesses, making money on the side and, in a growing number of cases, quitting their jobs to commit themselves fully to their own brand. All a person really needs to attract clients is access to the Internet. That, combined with the growing desire, particularly by the newer generations, to not be **stuck in** the traditional **9 to 5 lifestyle**, is resulting in a huge shift in the way that people work. They want to have freedom to work from home, from the cafe, from the beach or from the other side of the world; and they want to be their own bosses.

Everybody is on social media and everybody uses search engines when they need to know more information about any given topic. That means that, for business owners - be it traditional ones or the entrepreneurs and freelancers I just talked about - it is absolutely crucial to invest in **Digital Marketing** efforts, and both Social Media Marketing and SEO are two of the biggest components of that area.

Social Media Marketing is a form of Digital Marketing that, just like the name suggests, consists of any efforts you put into the usage of social media platforms such as Facebook, Instagram and Twitter, to promote a business and increase traffic and leads. Different businesses have different goals, needs and customers, and that translates into the type of platforms that are more advantageous for them, but I will dive into that later in the e-book.

SEO stands for Search Engine Optimization and it consists of the efforts invested towards improving a website's organic traffic on search engines. In other words, working on your SEO means working on your website so that, when a user searches for certain keywords that you define, your website will appear, at least, on the first Search Engine Result Page (SERP) - and, of course, the ultimate goal is for your web page to be the first one on the list of results.

If you have a business or are starting one in 2019, there is no doubt about whether or not you should invest in these areas, and statistics from previous years prove so:

- The Global Digital Report 2018, by We are Social and Hootsuite, states that in 2017, over **4 billion people worldwide used the internet** and a little over **3 billion were**

active social media users (you should also consider the fact that these numbers have been continuously increasing over time so, as I write this e-book they should be bigger and, as you read it, even bigger). The same report showed that, in January of 2018, each person spent an average of **6 hours a day using "internet-powered devices and services"** (Kemp, 2018) and that, although the distribution of Internet is not yet balanced, countries with low penetration rates have seen a **fast and continuous growth on their Internet usage**.

- According to The 2018 Sprout Social Index: Realign & Redefine report, 60% of consumers want to know about **new products and** services on social media, 59% are interested in educational posts, 56% in entertainment, and 49% in inspirational posts.

- 58% of users prefer visual content, which comes as no surprise, since the human brain processes images 60 000 times faster than text (Elsenberg, 2014).

- 45% of consumers use social media for customer service purposes.

- During 2017, for each second that went by, there were 11 new social media users. Crazy, isn't it?

- In 2017, users spent almost 1.5 trillion dollars on e-commerce.

For someone who owns a business but who's not familiar with Digital Marketing, Social Media Marketing might seem like something really easy to handle, while SEO might seem like the complete opposite. As you will understand throughout this e-book, neither of those is necessarily true. However, before you even think about your digital presence, your brand needs to be well settled - and that is exactly what I will talk about in the next chapter.

Chapter 2: Building a Personal Brand in 2019

A business is a commercial enterprise, but behind every business there is an individual and now more than ever, people want to get to know and connect to those individuals. That is the big reason why it is so important to have a personal brand. And that applies to those who already have an established business, as well as for those who are just starting one.

So your personal brand differs from your business brand, in the sense that it is about you as an individual - you are the product being marketed, so to speak. It is a person who communicates with your audience and who shows your ideals, opinions and values more than a business brand would. In other words, a personal brand is more human: it is about putting a face to the product/service and allowing customers to relate to it, turning your brand into more than just a source of sales.

As you read this you might start feeling a little bit discouraged because you are not a celebrity and getting followers and visits is not that easy. Well, the key to success is a positive attitude! Keep in mind that you are still a person with expertise and knowledge to share and that the goal is not to reach the entire world, but the people who make up your business brand's audience target.

Benefits of Creating a Personal Brand

You build a connection with your customers, and they see you and your brand as trustworthy

It is just like building a relationship with a new friend. First you get to know them, you keep interacting and learning more about their opinions and, after a while, *voilá*, you have a new person in your life who you know you can trust.

With the proper work being done, the same thing can happen between your personal brand and the customers. People will start remembering your name and your face. Because you are an actual person - and not just a logo or a slogan - consumers can feel an emotional connection with you and, with time, they start trusting you, which will reflect on the performance of your business brand. You may even become a thought leader in your industry, which is the quintessence of trust.

It is a great way of growing your network

If the efforts you put into your personal brand go well, you will start gaining followers online, that is, other people who want to keep up with what you have to say on your digital platform profiles. Among those followers, you will find a lot of people who are your current clients and want to keep up with the news, as well as some prospect customers.

In addition, there will also be people interested in collaborating with you and/or people who work in the same industry and who can be great contacts to have on your contact list. And the great thing is that, once your personal brand is well established, this networking process will become automatic, the follower count, the mentions and the direct messages will come to you and all you have to do is reply to the ones that seem interesting. You will not have to do all the work that goes into networking. And, as an entrepreneur, we bet you know how difficult finding new contacts can be!

It gives more visibility not only to your brand, but to yourself as a professional

A personal brand is one more channel to promote your product or service, so it is clear why having one can increase the visibility of what you are selling. When you put yourself out there as the owner of business XYZ, people get to see a part of the brand that they haven't seen before: the person behind it. And a person can be so much more than a business owner! So, having your own personal brand and working on it can get you to a point where you start having access to more (and more diverse) career paths that maybe you would not find with just a business brand. For instance, it is not uncommon for people with successful personal brands to be invited to speak at conferences or teach workshops about their area of expertise.

More Sales

The combination of the four benefits mentioned above - the trust, the connection, the new contacts and the visibility - will increase your product or service exposure, make your audience grow and, ultimately, translate into the bigger goal: more sales!

Chapter 3: Building Your Core Brand Strategy: 5 Tips for Success

After reading the benefits on the last chapter, you may be interested in building your own personal brand. Just like with a business brand, doing so is all about strategy. Once you have your core strategy settled, nourishing your personal brand will become more and more natural to you. Here are some tips to build your core personal brand strategy:

1. **Be yourself**. This is key to a successful personal brand, because it helps you maintain a consistent image. Otherwise you will have the extra work of having to keep up with the lies you tell your audience and, as good as those lies may make you

look in the beginning, it will never be worth it. The truth always comes up and you will not only have a lot of explaining to do, but you will lose the trust your followers put in you. Everyone prefers authenticity and that is what will bring you the type of followers you want to reach.

Now, that does not mean you cannot change your opinions - it is human nature to do so. Just be honest about it. Just because you post something today, it does not mean that you have to defend that stance for the entire time you have an online presence. People change and grow, and followers will understand that, as long as it comes from a place of sincerity towards yourself and them.

All of this means that you have to know who you are. You might tell me, "Of course I know who I am!" But do you know how to use that to market yourself? The next chapter is all about identifying who you are and using that to design your offer, so don't worry, I will help you with this tip.

2. **Choose your target**. This one comes hand in hand with the previous tip. Being authentically yourself means you will not appeal to everyone - and that is not the goal anyway!

Consider your area of expertise, your communication style, the message you want to convey and your overall goal with this brand. By doing so, you will find the niche of people you want to reach. Having a clear idea of who you want to talk to will makes things a lot easier when the time comes to actually do the talking.

Write down the target audience you want to reach with your personal brand.

3. **Be an expert.** You are probably a good professional in the industry you work in. The difference between a good professional and an expert lies particularly on the process of continuous learning. Become an expert by keeping up to date with everything going on within said industry. You can do so by reading magazines and books, by listening to podcasts, by following relevant pages on social media, by keeping in touch with other people within your niche - all you need to do is find

your method(s) to make sure you are consistently updated.

And, of course, only say something when you have something meaningful to say. Talking about a situation just to say you did will not help you become a relevant voice; you will just be another person on the Internet.

Write down the sources you will use to update yourself.

4. **Have a visual side to your brand.** We have mentioned before how important visuals are in the

online universe. Having a logo, a website and even business cards with consistent, top quality design makes you automatically look more attractive to potential customers and partners. Don't worry if you are not a designer, this is a task you can definitely outsource.

And on the topic of visuals, when you use photos of yourself, go for high quality ones, that will appeal to your target (which should not be hard, if you follow tip number one).

5. Take time to regularly work on your website, as well as on your social media profiles. I will let you know how later in the e-book!

Chapter 4: Identifying Yourself & Creating Your Offer

I have highlighted the importance of being honest and authentic before. It is impossible to do that if you don't know yourself and a good way of working on it is by answering some self analysis questions.

1. *What is my area of expertise and what can I offer to my audience?*

2. *What are my strengths and my weaknesses as an individual?*

3. *What are my strengths and my weaknesses as a professional?*

4. *How do I deal with big obstacles?*

5. *What is my biggest goal in life?*

6. *Which skills do I still need to work on to achieve that goal?*

7. *What type of people do I usually get along with easier in "real life"?*

8. *If I was someone else, why would I follow myself on social media?*

9. *What are my biggest passions?*

10. *How would those around me describe me?*

Now that you have answered these questions, you probably have a better sense of self. Summarize and compile the information you have written down and try to understand how you can use it to market yourself and to acquire more skills through a personal brand. If it makes it easier, you can even write it down as if you were describing someone else, as such: "[Your name] is a [your professional], with expertise in [...]," and so on.

You can write down your notes below.

Chapter 5: Instagram Marketing For Your Brand in 2019

Instagram is a visual social media mobile app, where the user's profile is composed of photos and videos, and the feed shows all the photos and videos posted by the people who the user follows (ordered by an algorithm, instead of chronologically like it used to be). Instagram also has a temporary content component: the Instagram Stories, but it has evolved so much during the last few years that I believe it deserves a chapter on its own, which is the next one.

Instagram has been around for almost a decade, but it has become especially popular during the past couple of years (although in the beginning, it gained an incredible amount of one million users in just three months of existence, and all organically!). And rightly so: if you recall, the human brain processes images way faster than text. Visual is easy and that is what people want when they log in to their social media.

In 2012, Instagram was bought by Mark Zuckerberg, the founder of Facebook, so the two platforms can easily be connected and managed side by side, which will definitely make your job easier, but I will get into that later.

Today, Instagram is the number one photography app, that is used by all kinds of people: from the individual who just wants to take amateur photos of his or her daily life, to the professional photographer who only posts high quality visuals. It is available for both Android and iOS, so you do not need a specific device to create your profile; and you can also access it on your computer, although the functionalities are limited (it is more of a solution for desperate times, like if you ever lose or break your phone).

Personal Account vs. Business Account

You can choose to have a personal profile or a business one (note: you need to have a Facebook page to be able to change your account to business). The main differences are that with a business account:

- You have access to the analytics, that is, to how each of your posts and your profile in general are performing. So this means profile visits, interactions, post impressions, demographic information of your followers, and more. Note, however, that Instagram only starts gathering this data once you change your profile type; you will not have access to any of your previous posts' performances.

- You can add your email address and/or your contact number and/or your location on your profile (that will be clickable and more noticeable than if you simply had them on your bio).

- You can promote your posts and create ads.

Making an Instagram Post

When you want to post a photo or video on

Instagram, you need to click on the "plus" icon that appears on the bottom of the app. Before, Instagram only used to post square photos and, if you tried to post a horizontal or vertical one, it would make you crop it to have a 1:1 ratio. However, in 2015 that changed and Instagram started accepting both landscape and portrait posts.

For your square photos, the optimal size is 1000 pixels by 1000 pixels and for landscape, it is 1080 pixels by 1350 pixels. Regarding the portrait photos, use a height of 1080 pixels and whatever width corresponds to that, so that your photo does not lose quality.

Each post can have up to 10 photos and or videos. After you choose those, Instagram will show you its own photo filters - although a lot of people use other apps for the editing process - and as well as some internal tools that you can use to fix your images there, in case you need to change the brightness or the contrast, for example. You can choose to add a location to your post (which is clickable and leads the user to a map), to tag other users and to add a caption, where you can include hashtags, a very popular part of this social app. Then, all you need to do is click "Publish," and you can also choose to post the same photo in four other social platforms: Facebook, Twitter, Tumblr, and Flickr. If you do so, people will be able to see that you originally posted the image on Instagram and they will have the option to go to your Instagram profile from that one post, so it can be a good way for you to gain more followers there.

In terms of interactions, you can like, comment and share other people's posts. There is also an Explore page, with posts by people who you don't follow but who might be of your interest. These posts are chosen automatically by Instagram according to your behavior in the app.

Instagram Ads

Everything I talked about before refers to organic posts, but, as I mentioned when I was talking about the option of having a business account, there is also the option of advertising on Instagram, which became available in 2013. There are four types of ads you can choose from:

- **Photos or Videos**: they both look like organic posts, except they have a call-to-action (CTA) at the bottom of the visual and a link to an external page. The video can have a maximum of 60 seconds.

- **Carousels**: they can have up to 10 pictures or videos (of 60 seconds max, altogether) in the same post. This type of ads is awesome for creative storytelling or showcasing of products or services and it also includes a CTA and a link.

- **Slideshow**: it is kind of like a video in the sense that it can have audio. However, instead of it being a continuous action, the post is made by a series of static slides that show up one after another.

- **Story**: this one I will talk about in more detail in the next chapter.

Instagram Statistics from 2017 and 2018

Users & Interactions

- By the end of last year, Instagram had more than 500 million active daily users (Clarke, 2019). There are over 1 billion accounts on it (Clarke, 2019).

- 60% of the users go on the app every day. The average amount of time that a user under 25 years old spends on Instagram is 32 minutes (Clarke, 2019). For those over 25, it is a little bit less: 24 minutes (Clarke, 2019).

- By December of 2018, 4.2 billion likes were happening on a daily basis (Clarke, 2019).

- By December of 2017, there were 25 million business accounts (Alsman, 2019).

- In terms of demographics, 71% of users are under 35 years old (Clarke, 2019). The adults who do use it tend to have higher incomes (Clarke, 2019). When we speak about user locations, the United States, India and Brazil are the countries with the biggest amount of followers (Clarke, 2019). Gender wise, 68% of the users are females (Alsman, 2019).

- There is a 2.2% interaction rate (Clarke, 2019).

Content & Hashtags

- Up until September of 2018, over 50 billion pictures had been shared on Instagram (Alsman, 2019).

- In that same month, there were over 100 million photos and videos being uploaded daily (Alsman, 2019).

- #love, #instagood and #me were the top three most popular hashtags in 2018 (Alsman, 2019).

- Posts with at least one hashtag get an average of 12.6% more engagement than hashtag-free posts (Alsman, 2019).

Ads

- ¼ of the ads on Instagram are on video format (Agrawal, 2019).

- When it comes to engagement on promoted posts, videos perform better than photos (Agrawal, 2019).

- There are 2 million monthly advertisers on the platform (Clarke, 2019).

Personal Branding on Instagram in 2019

Anyone who is on social media has heard the term "Instafamous." It refers to the people who have gained a big amount of followers and became particularly popular on the platform. They are like the celebrities of Instagram. These are people who have thrivingly built a personal brand on the app. Don't worry if your goal is not to become a celebrity per say: you can use these tips and look at "Instafamous" people's strategies for inspiration, so you can become a personal brand of reference in your own area of expertise.

Understand if it makes sense for your brand to have an Instagram account

Instagram might be a great social app for everyone, even if at first it seems like you don't have that much visually appealing content to show. For some, it is pretty obvious: if you do something that is inherently visual, like makeup or tattooing, if you have a brand where you make beautiful products, like jewelry or clothes, or if you are really good at something that makes beautiful pictures, like yoga or baking - you should definitely be on Instagram.

For others, it is not that clear. If you have more to say than you have to show, you might not see Instagram as something worth working on. However there are options that can make your account stand out, like if you work on designing cool infographics with the information you want to share or if you go for the short video format. But, the keypoint here is that you have to be willing to invest your time and efforts to make great content. If you are not... you might want to go for a more text-based social platform (can you think of one? I will talk about it soon!).

Set a goal for your account and make a strategic plan for it

So you decided Instagram is for you. Now it is time to think about what you want to achieve with your profile. Do you want to become a thought leader? To promote your business brand? To network? All of the above? If you have a business, you are aware of the importance of clearly knowing your end goals, so I will not get into that. Any professionally-related social media you start is no exception to that rule.

You can find an example of a simple strategic plan on page 62 of this ebook so, after you are done reading it, consider filling it out, even if it is just a first draft.

Opt for a business account

You already know the benefits of having a business account. What you might not know is how you can turn yours into one. It is pretty simple: all you need to do is go into your Settings and choose "Switch to Business Profile." Then, you will have to log into your Facebook account, connect it to one of your pages (that is why you need a Facebook page to have a business account) and add at least one contact to your page. And you are good to go!

Make sure you make the most out of the top part of your profile

By "top part" we mean your profile picture, you bio and your contact info. This is the first thing a user sees when they click on your profile so it should not only make an impact, but give them a clear idea of what kind of account you are. So:

- Don't underestimate your profile photo. Yes, it is small, but everyone *notices* it and it appears on each action you take on Instagram. If you use a photo of yourself, pay attention to details like the quality, of course, and if people can actually can see what you want to show. If you use a photo where you are too far away, people will not be able to actually see you, because Instagram's profile picture is so small. You can experiment and try out different photos until you find the best one for that size.

- Write a bio that goes with the kind of content you will be posting. Think of it as what sets the tone for what the user will see once they start scrolling down your profile. You can also add your name on top of the bio and, since you are marketing yourself, it is a good idea to actually use your real one (or artistic one - whatever you want people to refer to you as). Under you bio, you can have a link to an external page, so choose a relevant one, like your business brand's website or to another one of your social media profiles.

- Don't forget to add your phone number and/or you email. If someone sees your profile and wants to contact you, they are simply one click away. There is no need for them to try and research how they can get a hold of you, which can (and probably will) greatly increase the chances of people contacting you.

Build a visually appealing profile

One that will make people go "Wow!" when they open it , that shows that you put in time to manage your Instagram, instead of posting just anything. A good way of doing so is by defining a theme for your feed and applying it to all your photos. This means choosing a specific filter, a set of colors that predominate and a style of photos. Besides giving your profile a more organized look, opting for a theme also makes your job easier, since you always do the same process for each photo. After a while, it becomes almost automatic. When there is something you really, really want to share but that does not meet your profile's standards, you can always post in on your Stories (see next chapter).

Don't go too crazy on the hashtags

No one likes a post with a million hashtags on it, especially when they are not related to the post or to a person's niche, which happens quite often. It makes you look like you are trying too hard, which is never a good look. Plus, it makes it seem like you just want followers, instead of relevant followers. It does not look professional.

But, that also doesn't mean that you should not use hashtags at all. Remember how many photos are posted on Instagram every single day? You have to take every chance to make yours catch the eyes of the right people. It is a matter of balance, consistency and strategic thought. You can use external apps to help you understand which hashtags you should add to your post: Iconosquare is a popular example.

Follow and engage with the right people

It is a quick and easy way of making connections and getting noticed by other people's followers (remember you want to make a good impression, so think before you like or comment on a post). Furthermore, it is a great way of constantly getting updates on your industry.

When you find people you would like to partner up with or simply talk to, don't hesitate to send them a direct message. The more followers they have, the smaller the chances of you getting noticed, but the reality is that you never know. The online is today's big way of networking and, with so many people on it, the best bet is to take chances and hope for the best. Naturally, you should try to write an appealing message that will make the other person want to reply, and that is not too long - time is precious and no one wants to spend it reading interminable messages. If you do end up getting noticed, that can culminate into awesome collabs and partnerships and ultimately in your name becoming more popular in the right niche, so you really don't lose anything by at least giving it a go.

For Inspiration: an Instagram Branding Success

When you do a research for best Instagram accounts, James Charles is a name that probably appears in every single result page.

James is a makeup artist and that is easy to understand as soon as you open his profile. He is not exclusively on Instagram, but it is where his journey to stardom began and his numbers there are amazing. Just look at that follower count!

He is already an established social media personality/beauty guru, so at this point he does not have to try as hard to get followers or connect with important people in the world of makeup. But to get there, he had to put in a lot of work - even he says, if you watch some of his videos, that he is quite addicted to working. James Charles started as just a kid posting makeup looks online and ended up becoming the first male ambassador of the huge makeup brand that is Cover Girl. All through the power of social media!

Let's take a look at his profile:

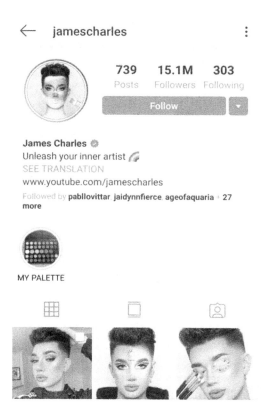

- His profile picture is not only high quality, but it is really creative and conveys perfectly what he does.

- His bio is simple, but clearly related to his area (and it includes an emoji, which always makes a bio more fun).

- He has a link to his YouTube channel: another social platform where he is extremely popular.

When you scroll down to his feed, you can tell that he puts a lot of thought into it:

- Most of his posts are of him showcasing his makeup skills.

- All the photos are high quality and beautifully edited, which gives the feed a very clean look.

- You can see he has become so popular, that he has the opportunity of doing collaborations with other social media personalities and celebrities.

Chapter 6:Instagram Stories

"Instagram Stories" is a functionality of Instagram, but it has become so popular that you can define a whole strategy just for it. When Instagram Stories was first introduced, you could post a photo and it would be available for your followers for 24 hours, but today you can post a lot more than that (and it is also available for those 24 hours):

- Type: if you just want to share text.

- Music: if you want to share a song.

- Live: if you want to do a livestream.

- Normal: a photo or a video (with a maximum of 15 seconds).

- Boomerang: a video on loop, with no audio.

- Superzoom: a Boomerang which can have several different effects, like one with hearts and a romantic song playing, or one that zooms in on what is being recorded and plays a dramatic audio.

- Rewind: a video on rewind.

- Hands-free: option to make a video without having to keep pressing the record button for it to keep recording.

On your story, you can:

- Use selfie masks and AR filters (created by Instagram, as well as by other users), that you can access by clicking the little face with sparks on the top of the screen, before you take the photo (or video, or boomerang).

- Add text and stickers, that can be emojis, a clickable location, clickable tags to other profiles, clickable hashtags, songs (from Spotify), the time when you are posting, GIFs (from Giphy), a countdown and the temperature either on Celsius or Fahrenheit.

- Generate interactions using other types of stickers, by creating a poll, asking a question (there is a special feature for questions, it would not be just text) or an emoji slider.

- Draw on it with several different colors and pencil or pen styles.

Once your story is ready to post, you can choose to send it to your Close Friends - a group of people you have previously defined-, to a specific follower (or followers) or to all of them. During the 24 hours while the Story is up, you can check how many people have seen your post, as well as who, and you can delete it if you want to, but you cannot edit it.

Instagram Story Ads

Instagram Stories can also be promoted, which means that they can have a "Learn more" or "Swipe up" option, where you can add a link to an external page. After you post your Story Ad, you have access to some insights, a.k.a. its performance, a.k.a.:

- Interactions.

- Replies.

- Profile Visits.

- Website Clicks.

- Impressions.

- Navigation (Back: how many times a user tapped back to see the previous story; Forward: how many times a user tapped forward to see the next story; Next Story; and Exited).

In case you make an Instagram Story and want it to be available for your followers for more than 24 hours, but still don't want to make a whole post about it, you can use the "Highlight" feature. After your Story is up, if you view it, you can see that there is a small heart icon at the bottom right corner: that is the Highlight button. When you click it, you add a row of Stories between your bio and your posts, which you can organize by categories and which will be available for your followers to view until you choose to not have it highlighted anymore.

Instagram Stories Statistics from 2017 and 2018

- 500 million people on Instagram use Instagram Stories daily (Instagram Stories Ads, 2019).

- The most used filter on Instagram Stories was the one called "Heart Eyes" and the most used GIF was the one called "Heart Love Sticker" (Instagram Year in Review 2018, 2018).

- 15% to 25% of the users who view stories click the "Learn more" option on Story Ads (Slichnyi, 2018).

- In 2017, a third of the most viewed Stories were posted by businesses and one fifth resulted in a DM from an Instagram user (Bojkov , 2019).

Personal Branding on Instagram Stories in 2019

Investing on Instagram Stories can potentially be a great way of leveraging your Instagram account: it is fast, easy content and you can get really creative with it. Plus, it does not always have to be as perfect as an Instagram post, so it may even mean less work for you.

Show exclusive content

An example of exclusive would be the behind-the-scenes of what you do. Those who are interested in your final product will probably also be interested in the process of making it. Moreover, this is an opportunity to show your expertise and hard work. You can do it by posting a series of video stories or by doing a livestream. People don't expect the Stories to be as "perfect" as the posts, so don't be afraid of being real.

Use stories to make small announcements

If you decide to organize a contest, if you are going somewhere and you would like to meet up with people in your niche, if you are going to be at a certain event or if you are nominated for some sort of award. You can make whole posts about this type of things, but posting a Story is also a great way of talking about it. It is a little bit more human and you don't have to edit yourself as much.

Create a row of highlights

Highlighting some of your best stories makes a great little extra on your profile. You can organize it by category and put a little cover on each one, so that it looks better (you can use the Canva app to easily make these covers). For example, if you are a travel blogger, you can make one highlight grouping for each country or continent you visit and you can have each cover with the respective flag.

Ask questions

With stickers specifically developed to ask questions and make polls, it would be silly not to make the most of it, especially if one of your main goals on Instagram is to grow your network. People like sharing their opinions and it is always a plus if they feel like your Instagram is not 100% about you, but that you also want to listen to what they have to say.

Chapter 7: Facebook

The technology giant; probably the first one that comes to mind when we talk about social media. The number and variety of features on Facebook seems to be never ending and sometimes it is hard to keep up. However, there are some basics that can definitely be useful to grow your personal brand and, when big updates happen, everyone ends up knowing about it, either because Facebook lets its users know or because it becomes a conversation topic. So you don't need to be a Facebook pro to make the most of it, you just need to keep an eye open for new updates that can be interesting for you to explore.

Personal Profile vs. Business Page

For your personal brand, you can choose between a Profile or a Facebook Page. A Profile has a limit of how many people can connect with you (although once your friend limit is reached, people can choose to "Follow" you), but it also makes it easier for you to control who is in your little Facebook networking circle and it gives a more human feel to your brand. With a Facebook Page you don't have that much control: once someone likes your page, they become your follower and you don't have a say about it, unless you end up blocking them, but that will probably only happen if that specific follower causes any problems on your profile. However, less control also (and the fact that there is no limit to the number of people who can't connect with you) means that your reach potential is a lot bigger.

So, choosing between these two is a matter

of you weighing in what you can do with each. And if you cannot choose, you can even have both and tailor it to different audiences within the same audience: for instance, you can have your Profile for people in the industry who you know and that you meet along the way, and the Page for other people who are interested but who you don't actually know. Just make sure that the two are consistent: you are still the same person managing and posting on both.

If you opt for a Profile, you can turn your current one into a Personal Branding one or you can create a second account solely for branding purposes, by following the same steps you did to create your personal one. One thing you should pay special attention to with a Profile is the privacy settings of each of your posts. I will go into more detail about privacy in a few paragraphs.

A Facebook Page is like a profile, but instead of it being personal and only for people you know, it is public, anyone can follow it and you use use it to show your brand. When you create a Page, you can choose between two types: Business or Brand (for business pages) and Community or Public (for non-business pages, such as a fan account). After you choose one of those, you will need to put in your Page Name (choose wisely because you will not be able to change it), to select a Category and, in some cases, to add your address and/or your phone number.

Afterwards, Facebook will give you the chance to add your Page's profile and cover photos or videos, but if you don't have them at that point, you can skip these steps. And that is it, your page is created. But of course, there is a lot more to edit and add.

- **Username**: that will be at the end of your page's URL and will make it easier for people to find you.

- **Page Info**: start date and business type.

- **CTA**: related to your business (so if you had a restaurant, for example, you could choose the one to make a booking).

- **Interests**

- **More info**: release date, about, biography, awards, gender, menu (in case of restaurants) and more.

- **Story**: like a blog post about your brand's story, that can also have a cover photo.

- **Team members**: where you can

add your personal profile, if you would like.

- **Services**

- **Community**: in case you also have a Facebook group related to your brand.

Facebook Pages have 10 templates available (Shopping, Business, Venues, Movies, Nonprofit, Politicians, Services, Restaurants & Cafes, Video Page and Standard), that automatically customize certain details of your page accordingly. When your profile is all prepared, with all the important info and visuals, you are ready to start posting and your posts can be organic or promoted. In terms of engagement and interactions, people can like, comment and share your posts, talk to you privately on Messenger and leave reviews.

Just like on Instagram, here too you can post Stories, but this functionality is not nearly as popular and used on Facebook. When you post a Story on Instagram, there is an option to also share it on Facebook, so you can keep your Facebook Stories active with zero extra work.

Facebook Statistics from 2018

- Facebook has almost 1.5 billion active daily users on mobile, and 2.32 overall (Ahlgren, 2019).

- 85% of the people who have a smartphone use the Facebook app (Ahlgren, 2019).

- In May of 2018, there were 80 million Facebook Pages (Ahlgren, 2019).

- Every minute, 400 people start a Facebook account (Ahlgren, 2019).

- The age group that uses Facebook the most is between 25 and 34 (25%) (Top 20 Facebook Statistics – Updated March 2019, 2019).

- Every minute, there are 4 million likes happening on Facebook (Ahlgren, 2019).

- The organic reach of a post is 6.4% of the page's followers (Bain, 2019), and the number has been decreasing continuously.

- Videos get an average engagement rate of 6.01% (Cooper, 2018).

- 150 million users were using Facebook Stories in 2018 (Cooper, 2018)..

Personal Branding on Facebook in 2019

Facebook is that one social platform that you just cannot ignore - after reading those statistics you probably understand why. Naturally, the strategy you should opt for depends on why you are using Facebook. These tips, for instance, are useful for those using Facebook for Personal Branding.

Fill in all the relevant information

Facebook has so many different fields in the "About" section, that you need to make the most of them to be in control of what you want the people to know about you and to promote your personal brand as you want. Things like your education, your professional experience, any certifications or awards you have won: people might try and look that up online and nothing is more reliable than the information available on your own profile or page. Most people are curious and they will end up clicking on the "About" section on your profile, so don't disappoint them. And don't forget to keep updating it as your career grows, of course.

Besides this, you should have at least one contact for anyone who might want to chat with you (one that you actually use - if someone tries to get in touch and simply gets ignored, they will build an unfavorable image of you. That is as easy to avoid as having an email address solely for contact inquiries and making sure you get notifications from new emails). You might think this is not that important, because if people want to talk to you they can just send you a message through Facebook

Messenger. Sure, you might be right and never get an email from a Facebook contact, but that is the kind of thinking that might make you lose interesting opportunities. Remember that a lot of personal branding relies on networking, so you should not miss any potential opportunity to meet new people in your industry.

If you are using a Personal Profile, pay attention to your privacy settings

Pages are inherently public, so if you are using one to promote your personal brand, you don't need to worry about privacy settings. However, that is not the case with Personal Profiles. You can manage these settings on two levels: your whole profile and each post.

Profile Privacy Settings

Go on your profile's settings and choose "Privacy," from the list of options on the left. There you will find a few privacy settings and tools and below I will list the ones you should pay attention to. These will be the standard settings for anything you do on your profile:

Your Activity

- "Who can see your future posts?" - Here you should choose the "Friends" option, so that the content you post is exclusive for your Facebook community. You might be wondering what would lead people to send you a friend request if they cannot see anything you post beforehand, but remember that these are the standard settings. Soon we will see the privacy settings for each post, which you can strategically use to have some teasers posts, that will make the right people want to know more and, hopefully, want to add you to their network.

- "Review all your posts and things you're tagged in" - For safety reasons, you should activate the option to manually review everything you are tagged in. Just in case you get tagged in spam posts or a friend confuses this profile for your actual personal one and tags you in a photo from last weekend's wild night. This way you are 100% in control of what can and cannot appear in your profile.

How People Find and Contact You

- "Who can send you friend

requests?" - Set this to "Everyone" and then decide who you want to accept or not as your Facebook friend. There are spam accounts and trolls on Facebook, which you will not want in your online network.

- "Who can look you up using the email address you provided?" and "Who can look you up using the phone number you provided?" - You will want to be found by relevant people, so definitely set both of these to "Everyone." You will probably give out your email and your phone number in several occasions and people might use those contacts to try and find you online.

- "Do you want search engines outside of Facebook to link to your profile?" - This is a no-brainer: you definitely do. Someone might have heard your name and a little bit about yourself and got an interest in what you do, so they try to google your name and boom, there it is, your own Facebook page, where they can find out more about you and even contact you. It is a winning situation for both people!

Besides this, everytime you post something, you can choose the privacy settings for that specific post. Before you hit "Share," click on the scroll down options next to "News Feed" right below what you have just written. Go for:

- **Public,** for those teaser posts I have mentioned before. If you believe a post could make a person want to connect with you, and if is not too exclusive, make the post public (i.e., anyone on or off Facebook can see it). Something like a contest you will be organizing or an event you will be speaking at can be good posts to have as public.

- **Friends,** for all the other posts. People sent you a friend request to see valuable, interesting content, so that is what you you should strive to give them.

- **Friends except...,** just in case you don't want a specific friend (or list of friends) to see a post.

Share your expertise

Unlike Instagram, Facebook is not inherently visual; it also includes quite a bit of text. Now, that does not mean that posting mostly text is the way to go: if you want to achieve the best possible results, you should accompany your text with good visuals (more on that on the next section). But since you can share a lot more words on Facebook, it is a great chance to show your knowledge to your followers in more detail.

If you have a blog, for instance, you should always share a link to your new blog posts. If you were interviewed or had a guest post somewhere, you should do the same thing. See, the actual long content is not on Facebook, but since it is so easy to share posts like this on the platform, it is definitely something you should not ignore. People who are interested in what you have to say will click, especially if your post has a good, compelling copy and if the snippet shows optimization for social media sharing.

Post with good quality and consistent imagery

You should do this for every visual piece you use:

- **Profile picture**: besides the usual quality standards, make sure you use a photo with the right dimensions that, in this case, are 2048 pixels by 2048 pixels (remember that, even though you will upload a square image, Facebook will crop it into a circle).

You should give out a professional and trustworthy vibe, which can mean different things for different industries and niches -- it does not necessarily need to be you in a suit or a work dress. If you want to establish yourself as a fitness expert, for example, you should have a picture of yourself wearing good quality fitness attire. You can even hire a professional photographer or ask a photographer friend to take these photos for you. If you cannot afford the first one and don't have the second one, my tip is that you go on entrepreneur and freelancing related Facebook groups and ask if there is any photographer in your area who would like to do a service swap: in this case, a photography session for a workout session would be a great offer. You will probably find someone up for it! Both of the parties would benefit from this and it could even be a great opportunity to create some word-of-mouth.

- **Cover photo**: your cover photo can simply be a good photo that relates to your area of expertise, but it can also be a great way of highlighting something you want to announce, like the release of a new product or an event you will be hosting.

If you choose to use your Cover Photos to make announcements, make sure your images have a nice design. If you have the means for it, you can outsource the design of your visuals or you can even make it a one time job, if you pay for a template that you can then edit yourself whenever you need to. Otherwise you can use Snappa and make the images yourself. Whatever you choose to post, don't forget to use the right dimensions: 1640 pixels by 720 pixels.

- **Post images**: these are the images that go with the posts that you make. They can be photos or designed images. What matters for these images is the width, that should be 476 pixels; the height can vary.

One thing to keep in mind is that, if you use text in your design images, you need to remember that a lot of people go on Facebook through their mobile device. So, when it is time to design these visuals, make sure they will be readable even on the phone. In other words, what I am saying is that the font cannot be too small.

- **Link preview image**: when you write a URL in the "What's on your mind, [insert your name]?" section, a snippet appears and, in that snippet, there should be a horizontally oriented image.

If you are posting a link to your website or blog, you should make sure that all your pages have this image with the optimal dimensions, which are 600 pixels by 314 pixels. You can do this by going on your website's back office, going to the Edit page of whatever you are trying to share and look for the "Social Media" section. Try and do this whenever you publish a new page on your website and you will not have to worry about it again.

- **Event image**: you may not use this one as often, but it is still good to know a couple of tips. Go for an image that is 1200 pixels by 675 pixels and, again, make sure that if you include text in the image, don't use a font that is too small, otherwise the readability for mobile will be compromised.

Note: the ideal dimensions for each of the images changes regularly, so try to keep yourself updated.

Reply to your messages on Facebook Messenger

If you do this whole personal branding on social media thing right, people will want to get in touch and you most likely will get several questions, recommendations and comments. It is quite important that you try your best to reply to, or at the very least acknowledge as many as you can. Leaving everyone on "Read" will give you the reputation of someone who is not approachable, which will translate into a big obstacle for the growth of your network.

In case you are using a Page for your branding, you can turn to Instant Replies to help you with this task. To use Instant Replies, go on your page and select "Settings." On the list of options on the left, you will find "Messaging," which is where you should click. On that page, there is a "Response Assistant" section and that is where you will be able to activate and personalize your Instant Replies, as well as scheduling times when people will get a message saying that you are not available and will get in touch soon. Set up a nice instant reply and then, when you can, take some time to look at the messages you got and message them back.

Chapter 8: Facebook Advertising

Just like on Instagram, Facebook also gives you the option to make organic posts or to invest on them (this only applies for Facebook Pages -- Personal Profiles cannot use Facebook Advertising). My advice is that you consider doing some ads, as there is more and more competition on Facebook everyday and the reach of organic posts on this platform (and on any other, in reality) has been continuously decreasing.

As a Facebook Page, there are two ways in which you can invest on your posts: you either make a regular post and then promote it, or you create ads. The truth is that a promoted post is a type of ad, but there are still some differences that you might want to consider when you need to choose between the two. When you boost a post, you just widen its audience, in hopes of achieving a result specific to said post. The Ads are bigger than that and involve a little bit more strategy and thinking. They can constitute a whole digital marketing campaign and include more advanced customization options.

Boosted Posts

To promote a post, write and publish it as you normally would and, after it is published, click on the option to "Boost Post." After accepting Facebook's non-discrimination policy (it exists to prevent ads from being discriminatory in terms of race, country, religion, age, sex, sexual orientation, gender identity, and others - something you should ALWAYS obey by), you will see a popup with some options for you to manage your boosted post (and you will also be able to preview your post both on desktop and on mobile, on the right side of the popup):

Audience

The group of people you want this promoted post to reach. You have three options here:

- People you choose through targeting: a group of people whose demographics (gender, age and locations) you define. As you change these demographics, Facebook shows you your post's potential reach, so you can experiment and try to reach a good number of people.

- People who like your Page (you can

change the Location to restrict or widen the audience within your followers).

- People who like your Page and their friends (again, you can change the location).

Budget and duration

- Total budget: the amount of money you want to spend, that will be distributed over the days you choose to have the post promoted (the minimum is one currency unit per day).

- Duration: you can have the promoted post running for one day, one week or two weeks.

- Under Budget and Duration,

Facebook lets you know the cost per day, according to the amount of money and the number of days you choose. No maths from your part needed here.

Payment

You will have a payment method connected to your Facebook Page, which will automatically appear in this section. However, you can change this.

Facebook Ads

The other Facebook Ads available are a little bit more complex than the Boosted Posts, but nothing too crazy. They are quite similar to the ones I described in the last chapter, since Facebook owns Instagram. To create ads, you need to go to Facebook's Business Manager, where you can create eight different types of ads:

- **Photo**: an ad that includes an image (with a ratio of 9:16 or 16:9) and a link, accompanied by a copy. The simplest and easiest one to put up.

- **Video**: an ad with a video that can be short (GIFs, vertical videos, a video carousel or a video collection) or long (in-stream video, i.e., those 5 to 15 second videos that play before you watch a video you clicked on).

- **Stories**: just like on Instagram, people can create and post Stories (the 24-hour only content) on Facebook. When you create a Story Ad, it will appear in between the user's others stories, posted by their friends, and it will give them the option to swipe up and learn more (again, just like Instagram).

- **Messenger**: ads that appear in a chat window between you and a user on Facebook Messenger. These ads are more personal, since "you" are talking one on one with the person on the other side of the screen, and they help start conversations with your potential customers. Messenger Ads can be fully automated. You create a quiz and, according to the person's answers, suggest the product or service that makes most sense. You can customize them to be as creative and interactive as you would like.

- **Carousel**: with carousel ads, you can have between two and ten photos or videos in the same ad and each of those can direct the user to a different link. You can order the slides yourself or let Facebook order them in an optimized way, according to their performance.

- **Slideshow**: similar to video ads, but presented in a slideshow format instead. You choose each image (which should have a ratio of 16:9, 1:1 or 2:3) or video for the slides, put them in order, choose the duration of each slide and, if you want, add music (and don't forget about the copyrights issue, otherwise your ad can end up being put down). When you build a Slideshow ad, make sure all the images have the same ratio; if they don't, Facebook will make them all 1:1 and parts of the images will be missed.

- **Collection**: these ads work like a catalog, where people can browse and find more about a brand's products. They include a main photo or video and then four smaller photos of whatever the brand wants to promote. There are four templates for Collection Ads, that you should choose depending on your end goals:

  o The Instant Storefront, if you want to show and sell four or more products;

  o The Instant Lookbook, if you want to tell a story and boost sales at the same time;

  o The Instant Customer Acquisition, for when you want to take the user to an app or website; and

- o The Instant Storytelling,
  when you want to tell a
  story.

- **Playables**: these are like a small
  trial. A Playable is an interactive ad
  where the user can try out an app
  before they download it. There are
  three components in a Playable ad:
  the initial video, that is an
  introduction to the app; the game
  demo, i.e., the interaction part; and
  the CTA, to lead the user to the app
  store.

Facebook Advertising Statistics 2018

- 26% of people who clicked on an ad

did make a purchase (Advertising with stories ads: Fast and immersive full-screen format | Facebook Business, n.d.).

- Facebook ads get, on average, an engagement rate of 3.91% (Advertising with stories ads: Fast and immersive full-screen format | Facebook Business, n.d.).

- 24.2% of pages invest on promoted posts and ads (Advertising with stories ads: Fast and immersive full-screen format | Facebook Business, n.d.).

- 58% of users have claimed that they would be more interested in a brand after seeing it on Facebook Stories (Advertising with stories ads: Fast and immersive full-screen format | Facebook Business, n.d.).

- 58% of people also said they have researched more about a brand after seeing it in a Facebook story (Advertising with stories ads: Fast and immersive full-screen format | Facebook Business, n.d.).

- 50% visited a brand's website, where they could make a purchase, after seeing their stories (Advertising with stories ads: Fast and immersive full-screen format | Facebook Business, n.d.).

- 31% went to a shop to have a look at a brand's products after seeing it in their stories (Advertising with stories ads: Fast and immersive full-screen format | Facebook Business, n.d.).

Facebook Advertising for Your

Brand in 2019

Follow Facebook's tips on which type of ad is recommended for your goal(s)

Facebook has conducted studies on their platform to understand how each format of ads works and you can find this information if you explore their Business blog, but here is a quick summary:

- Photo Ads are good if you want to take users to your website or raise awareness about a tangible product.

- Video Ads are a great choice if you want to capture the customer's attention more easily (just make sure your first 3 seconds are amazing even without sound and make the user want to click and watch more).

- Stories Ads work best if you want to create a quick, authentic ad experience for the user and if you want to efficiently drive a specific action on their end.

- Messenger Ads let you reach a huge amount of people, offer them an interactive ad experience and start conversations with potential customers.

- Carousel Ads are great for storytelling, for showcasing a new line of products or for describing in detail the features of one single product or service.

- Slideshow Ads work best if you need to make a complex story more clear or if you want to make sure even people with slow connections can watch your ad, without it having to be just one single image.

- Collection Ads are great to encourage sales.

- Playable Ads are the way to go if you want the user to give your app a try and, hopefully, end up downloading it.

Keep in mind that you are not selling a product (at least not directly), but yourself

If you were to promote a product or a service, your final goal would probably be to sell, so you would construct your Facebook Ad strategy around that. But here that is not the focus; at least, not your primary focus, since by promoting your personal brand you will be second-hand promoting your business brand. So, what do you want people to understand and do through your ad(s)? I would say for a personal brand, creating a video could be a really interesting choice, since it is most likely the most personal option Facebook gives you. And of course, you can invest in more sporadic posts, like the ones related to your future events or appearances in big conferences, if you think they are really worth spending your $$$.

Make your pennies count

Organic reach will not take you very far, so investing in Facebook Ads is always a good idea. However, as a personal brand, my advice is that you really take some time to define the audience you want to reach, as well as the duration of the ads, so that you do not end up wasting money. This is because you probably do not have the same kind of budget an enterprise would, so every penny counts.

Once you are done with those customizations, use creative ads either to lead the user to your personal website or to start a conversation with you on Messenger. Build those ads so that they will easily lead the person to take the action you want them to. As a one-person, low-budget brand, you don't want to make people have to do too much before they reach the finish line of your ad. So, when it comes to your call-to-action and the website linked to it, be straight to the point.

Try to make your ad not look like an ad

An ad is way more appealing if it does not look like one. So when you create your ads, do it as if you were going to publish a "regular" Facebook post. In Digital Marketing terms, this would mean going for native advertising, i.e., paid content that looks, feels and works like organic content, going with the flow of the platform you post them in. Don't try too hard, or it will not be as efficient as it could have been.

Chapter 9: Twitter

Twitter is a popular choice when it comes to promoting a personal brand (although its growth has slowed down over the last few years), where users can share short, straight to the point thoughts. Twitter was created in 2006 by Jack Dorsey, an American programmer who was, at the time, trying to create an SMS app. Little did he know that he would end up starting one of the most popular social media platforms of all time.

When someone visits your Twitter profile, they will see a cover photo, otherwise mentioned as header, that should be 1500 pixels by 500 pixels; your profile photo, which should be 400 pixels by 400 pixels (considering that Twitter will crop it into a circle); and your bio - a text of 160 characters maximum - followed by your location, website, your "twitterversary" (a.k.a. the date you created your Twitter) and your actual birthday. This info only appears if you choose to have it as public.

Twitter posts are called tweets. These used to have a limit of 140 characters but, by popular demand, two years ago that limit was increased to 280 characters. That means that Twitter users cannot write long content, which makes it very easy to digest. Along with the text, you can add up to four images (which should have a minimum of 600 pixels by 335 pixels), a GIF, a video or a link snippet. You can do basic edits to your photos (if you are tweeting from the iOS or the Android app), add up to 25 stickers to them and tag other users, as well as a location.

In terms of interactions, your followers can:

- **Retweet** your tweets, which is Twitter's version of "Share." When someone retweets your tweet, it will appear in their Twitter profile. They still appear as yours and that means that your audience for that post gets even bigger, which can be a great way of getting new followers. When someone retweets a tweet, they can also add a comment, which can spark conversations.

- **Like** your tweets.

- **Reply** to your tweets.

- Send you a **Direct Message** as a response to a tweet.

Under each of your tweets you will see three icons with a number to their right and they refer to three of these types of interactions: the speech balloon represents the replies, the two arrows represent the retweets, and the heart represents the likes. These numbers are visible not only to you, but to anyone who sees your tweets. There is also a little letter that users can click to send you a message, but that one does not have any number by it.

Twitter Ads

Similarly to the two social platforms I have talked about thus far, Twitter also gives its users the chance to create paid posts. To create Twitter Ads, you need to go on https://ads.twitter.com. After confirming your country and timezone, Twitter will ask you what goal you want to accomplish with your ad. It can be to:

- **Promote app installs**: when

creating this ad, you add the link to your app as well as the name. You pay for each click or install;

- **Get more followers**: you pay for each follower you gain;

- **Increase the engagement of your tweets**: you pay for the engagement created by the ad (so it does not include the engagement that might occur after you ad has run);

- **Get views on a video**: you pay for each view;

- **Take people to your website**: you pay for each click;

- **Make your app's current users open it and use it**: you pay for each click;

- **Publish videos along with premium content**: you pay for each view; or

- **Raise awareness through your tweet**: you pay for each impression.

For each ad campaign you create on Twitter, you can make ad groups and define their duration, the budget, the type of bid (there are three options that vary between types of ads: Automatic bid, where the budget is optimized for you to spend the least amount of money for the best possible results; Target cost, where you choose how much you want to pay, Twitter calculates the average per day you should achieve and you pay the average cost per action for each day; and Maximum bid, which allows you to choose how much you are willing to pay per action), your target's details and the creatives.

Depending on which goal you selected, your ad might appear in four different parts of Twitter: in people's feeds, in your own profile, on the search results page or on Twitter Audience Platform.

If you don't want the hassle of having to create campaigns and ads, Twitter gives you the option of automatically promoting your tweets for a monthly fee of $99. Not just any tweets though: they have to pass Twitter's quality policy. In other words, you have to have a functioning link on your bio that users can click on for more information, a profile picture and a header, your tweets should be clear and accurate, there should be a destination link, the text should be correct in terms of grammar and spelling and any images or videos should be good quality and be suitable for all users.

If you don't have time to create ads (and if

you have 99 dollars instead), this can be an interesting option, but keep in mind that there are no guarantees of a successful outcome.

Twitter Cards

Another functionality on Twitter is the Twitter Cards, that are like Tweets 2.0. They were initially created for people who had something to say that they could not put in just 140 characters, but they continue to be used even after that the character limit doubled. Twitter Cards can be a little bit tricky to create, since they involve some (simple) coding on your website's backoffice, so if you know a developer, consider asking them for their help; they will do it in no time. In case you have to do it yourself, Twitter provides useful resources and documentation on Twitter Developers and you can always check if they are correctly set up on Twitter Card Validator.

Once they are running, Cards have the potential to take your message even further than your profile: when users tweet a link the website you created a card for, a Twitter Card will appear and be visible to their followers.

There are four types of Twitter Cards:

- **Summary Cards** are composed of just text and they give the user a preview of the content they will see once they click the link on the card.

- **Summary Cards with Large Image** are exactly what you are thinking: a Summary Card with a clickable image attached to it. The image should have a ration of 2:1, a minimum of 300 pixels by 157 pixels and a maximum of 4096 pixels by 4096 pixels.

- **App Cards** promote mobile apps and they can include the name of the app along with its description, icon, rating, and price.

- **Player Cards** include video and audio and they are the most complicated ones to set up.

The Trending Section and Hashtags

If you go on Twitter's initial page, there is a section called "Trends for you." These are the most popular topics on the microblogging platform, according to your location, the accounts you follow and the tweets you post. You can search for other locations and the trends that appear will change. These trends are clickable and each of them takes you to a list of tweets that include said trend.

Some of the trends that appear in your profile will probably be hashtags. Hashtags are a big part of Twitter, since this was the platform they were first used in, and they can be a very useful way of widening your audience. When you put a '#' before a word or expression (with no spacing or punctuation), it becomes clickable and takes you to a list of tweets that include that hashtag.

Twitter Analytics

Everyone on Twitter has access to a part of

platform related to the Analytics of their tweets. This Twitter's sub-website includes five tabs of information about your performance.

Home

Shows you a summary with the highlights for each month that you are on Twitter: the top tweet of the month (the one with the most impressions), the top mention of your twitter handle (the one that gave you the most impressions), your top follower (the one that has the most followers), the top media tweet (your top tweet that includes an image, video or GIF) and the top tweet card (your card with the most impressions).

Tweets

Shows you a line graph of the impressions (number of times a tweet showed up on a user's feed) you got with your tweets during the month up to that point, as well as the totals of your engagement rate, link clicks, retweets, likes and replies you had on that period of time, and those same KPIs for each of your tweets.

Audiences

Shows you a bar graph of the evolution of your follower count. You can also choose to see the "All Twitter users" page, which gives you some insights on the users in the country: interests, demographics (such as education level, occupation, marital status and net worth), consumer behavior (buying styles and consumer goods purchases) and their mobile footprint (their wireless carrier).

Events

Shows you the events in several different categories and locations that people talk about the most on Twitter, with the amount of tweets about it, its total reach and impressions.

More

Includes analytics about videos you posted and about conversions you got to your website and/or your mobile app.

Twitter Statistics 2018

- In the last quarter of 2018, Twitter reached 321 million monthly active users worldwide (Top 10 Twitter Statistics – Updated March 2019 - Zephoria Digital Marketing, 2019).

- In 2018, there were 500 million tweets being posted daily (Cooper, 2019).

- From 2017 to 2018, ad revenue

increased by 25% (Top 10 Twitter Statistics – Updated March 2019 - Zephoria Digital Marketing, 2019.

- Twitter ads are 11% more efficient than ads that play during live events on TV (Cooper, 2019).

- The most popular emoji last year was the crying laughing one (Cooper, 2019).

- 46% of the people on Twitter use the app every day (Cooper, 2019).

- Tweets that include a video have an engagement 10 times higher than tweets without a video (Cooper, 2019).

- The biggest age group that uses Twitter is between 18 and 29 years old and represents 37% of the users (Aslam, 2019).

- US, Brazil, Japan and Mexico are the four countries with the most Twitter users (Aslam, 2019).

- 80% of the users go on Twitter through their phone (Aslam, 2019).

- 71% of the users get their news on Twitter (Cooper, 2019).

Personal Branding on Twitter in 2019

Twitter is a microblogging platform and microblogging can be done about any topic, which means that no matter what your area of expertise is, you can use Twitter to your advantage. Twitter is one of the most promising social media platforms for personal branding and there are countless successful cases of people with Twitter accounts that showcase its potential in promoting individuals and their careers. Those people probably followed these tips I am about to talk about!

Check your privacy settings

When you create a Twitter account, your tweets are public by default, which means that anyone, even people without a Twitter account, can read your posts. However, you can change your Privacy and safety settings, which will determine who can see and interact with your profile and the tweets you post. My suggestion is that you don't protect your tweets, your followers will not have the option to retweet them and you lose a great opportunity to increase your Twitter network. Moreover, if your tweets are protected, other users will not be able to find you through hashtags and trends (or outside of Twitter, through search engines) and if you reply to a tweet by someone who is not following you, they will not see it and that also negatively affects your chances of networking. What you want for your personal brand is the complete opposite of all of that.

Photo tagging, however, is a different story. For the same reason I mentioned when I was talking about other people tagging you on Facebook, I advise you to try and reduce chances of you being tagged in a post that negatively impacts your brand. Twitter does not offer the option to review each post you are tagged in like Facebook does, but you can choose to be tagged only by people who you follow. That does not 100% guarantee that you will never be tagged in a post that you don't want to be associated with, but it is less likely to happen (especially if you are "picky" about who you follow) and it makes the damage control a lot easier to manage.

Regarding Twitter Teams (a feature managed on TweetDeck, a tool created by Twitter to manage multiple Twitter accounts, track certain topics and hashtags, and organize your Twitter experience as you would like), also only allow people you follow to add you to their teams. This will prevent you from being added to teams that are not related to your area of expertise, while still allowing some people to be able to invite you into their groups. Since you are going to be promoting yourself, in the beginning you will probably not have to worry about Twitter Teams, but as time goes by and you become more influential, it will be useful for you to have these settings already defined as you will want them to be.

Take your time to choose a good Twitter handle

As well as fill in your information and add high quality imagery. Regarding your handle, it should be something easy to remember, that is related to you and what you do. Your first and last name would be the best option, but with the amount of Twitter accounts that exist nowadays, it is probably already taken (still try it though, you never know). Something you could do is add the letters of your middle name in the handle; so, if your full name was Carl Bergen Rogers and @carlrogers is already being used, you would try @carlbrogers. You could also create a handle that includes your name and something related to your brand: @alanatheyogi for Alana who practices yoga, @veganchef-tommy, for Tommy who is a vegan chef,

@vet_robert, for Robert who is a veterinarian - you get the idea.

Your bio should definitely contain a link to your website (especially if you are thinking about creating Twitter ads) and a short description, so that people understand right away what you are about, as soon as they go on your profile. For the images, just make sure you use the dimensions we recommended above (for those of you who forgot: it is 1500 pixels by 500 pixels for the header image and 400 pixels by 400 pixels for the profile photo), that they are good quality, and convey the image of someone who is really good in their area of expertise. These three things - your bio, profile photo, and header - are what the user first sees when they open your profile so it is important that you try to make a good first impression.

Follow the trends and hashtags related to your industry

The trends that show up for you probably also show up for people in the same area as you, and who have the same interests as you. Those people are also known as... the people you want to connect with! A great way of growing your personal brand is by keeping an eye on your trending topics. If you see that there is one that you can talk about (and by talk about, I mean say something relevant, that adds to the conversation), tweet away.

Doing so not only shows your followers that you keep up with what happens in the industry, but it has the potential to make your follower count go up. As you may remember, I mentioned that when you click on one of the trends in the list, it takes you to a list of tweets that include that hashtag. That means that if you use the hashtag, you too will be in that list. Of course, if the trend refers to something huge, like a globally known event, chances are a lot of people are talking about it and your tweet might end up getting lost in the middle of such a big conversation. An example of this would be the Web Summit. If you were already on Twitter when it happened, you probably noticed *everyone* was talking about it. It was very hard to stand out, unless you were a celebrity, a big technology thought leader or a speaker.

For that reason, you should not underestimate the power of the smaller events and trends related to your area of expertise. Those give you a way bigger chance of standing out, since not so many people will be talking about them. And if you think about it, when a trend or event is really specific to an industry, only people who are truly interested in it will talk about it.

But your use of hashtags should go beyond the trends. Studies conducted by Hubspot in 2018 have shown that tweets with hashtags can get up to 1,065% more engagement than tweets with no hashtags (Sabanty, 2019), so you should definitely include one to two hashtags on each of your tweets. To make sure you use the best ones, my suggestion is that you use a tracking tool that helps you find the top hashtags related to whatever you want to tweet about. Two good (and free) tools for that would be Tweet Binder and Twitter Search (Twitter's native search, available on "Advanced Search," on your profile).

One extra tip: include one hashtag in your profile bio. It is another way for you to get found by the right people, not only on Twitter, but also through search engines.

Follow the right people and interact with them

Personally, I find this one to be the most important thing to do in terms of personal branding on Twitter. You know who the thought leaders in your industry are and they probably have a Twitter account. Follow them as soon as you start your account (or if you already have one and don't follow them yet, make a pause on your reading, go on Twitter, hit those follow buttons, and then come back). If one of these thought leaders ends up following you back, make sure to DM them a well thought out message. They may or may not see it/respond to it, but it is only possible to message people who follow you on Twitter (unless they have their settings set so everyone can message them, but that option is more commonly used by business brands), so if you have the chance, take it.

Keep working on your Twitter network and follow a couple more relevant people every day (or as regularly as you can). Hopefully you will get those users' attention and start getting follow backs. It also works the other way around: keep an eye on people who follow you (as well as people who retweet or like your tweets -- anyone who appears on your notification page, really) and, in case you find someone who seems interesting for your personal brand, follow them back. And then, it is time to start the talking!

Don't let your Twitter profile be just a conversation between you and yourself, you will not attract anyone that way. You should reply to tweets by other people in your industry, pose questions to your followers and, if you want, you can even welcome people who give you a follow (maybe not everyone though, as it might turn into too much work, when your follower count starts growing more rapidly). Besides that, retweet and like other people's tweets!

Needless to say you should also try your best not to ignore any of your mentions. If you don't really have a reply for it, simply hit like and it will let the person know that you saw their tweet, which is the most important part.

Make a Twitter List (or more)

I have not talked about Twitter Lists yet, but they can be very, very useful for someone building their personal brand on Twitter. A Twitter List is like a Twitter feed, but only with the users you choose. You can have multiple lists for multiple topics and you can also keep updating them as you find more good accounts.

The reason this can be so useful is because, as you follow more people, the chances of you missing some more relevant tweets increases, since your feed gets updated more constantly. To make sure you don't miss anything, choose a few accounts that post the most informative, timely tweets and add them to a list. Then, make sure to check your lists everyday and, if there is anything worth talking about, do it.

If you get big on Twitter, you might even end up being the one who others add on their Twitter Lists. It is actually a great way of checking how much you are growing! You can access this information when you go on your own Lists: there you will find a section where you see which Lists you were added to.

For Inspiration: a Twitter Personal Branding Success Case

If you are a social media aficionado, you have probably heard the name Guy Kawasaki before. And if you are a social media aficionado who has a Twitter account, you are probably following him. Guy Kawasaki is not exactly a celebrity, but he sure is one of the top examples I could use as someone with a great personal brand on Twitter. Yes, maybe he has an advantage because he is a social media management expert and he has even given interviews on how to create a personal brand on social media. But hey, that also means that if you are looking for someone for inspiration, you can be certain that he is a great choice.

If you go on Guy's Twitter profile, you see right away that he follows a lot of the tips I mentioned above:

- His images are high quality and his cover photo is of him on the stage of a TEDx conference in Palo Alto. Can it get any more professional looking than that?

- His bio includes a small description of who he is and what he does, his location and his website.

- On Guy's feed, you will see that he retweets other people's tweets and sometimes uses hashtags (particularly the one he created to promote his book, #wiseguy. Creating hashtags for your own campaigns can be a great way of making it go even further, if it actually gets attention). Two other things Guy constantly does - that you too can do on your Twitter account - are curating content and retweeting his old tweets. By curating (high quality, relevant, and accurate) content, you become someone people go to to find out about the industry's updates. By retweeting some of your past tweets (the ones that performed the best when they were first posted), you can get more likes, retweets, and responses, increasing both your reach and your engagement.

- When you click on his likes, there are two things that are important to notice: the first one is that he likes tweets regularly. Not everyday, as I can imagine that Mr. Kawasaki is a busy man, but you will not find a bigger difference than four or five days between the likes. The second thing you should notice is that he doesn't just like tweets from verified accounts with a lot of followers; he also likes posts from people with just a few followers who mentioned his handle in their tweets. That makes him look very approachable, even as a social media guru with more than one million followers.

You can't see any information about Guy's Twitter Lists (a user's Twitter List page is only available to them), but I bet he has Lists that he regularly checks and that he is also on other people's Lists (a lot of them, probably).

Chapter 10: Youtube

YouTube is quite different from Twitter, Facebook and Instagram, because it focuses on one single format of content: video. Nowadays, YouTube is a really popular platform, with thousands of creators posting regularly and getting huge followings (and huge checks). It is so popular that it even led to the creation of a new profession - the YouTuber - and some of these YouTubers get so big that they end up becoming "traditional" celebrities and getting into acting, singing and/or hosting.

If you have a Gmail address, you already have a YouTube account, because both of those belong to Google, so they are connected, which means that you will not need to create a new account. However, there is still a lot to be done for you to be ready to start posting.

The 6 Tabs of a YouTube Profile

Each YouTube account has a profile page with channel art, i.e., a cover photo (that should be 2560 pixels by 1440 pixels) and a profile photo, which is the one you have set for your Gmail account and should be 800 pixels by 800 pixels as the dimensions. You can change it if you want to, keeping in mind that, if you change it on YouTube, it will also change on your email, and vice-versa. For the cover and the profile picture, follow the same suggestions I have given you for the other three platforms on this ebook: go for high quality and for a professional look that relates to what you do.

You should also make sure the imagery looks good for several different devices, but YouTube gives you a hand with that: when you choose the photo you want in your header, you will be able to see how it looks on a desktop, TV, and mobile, and adjust the crop for it to look good in all three options.

Home

A YouTube profile has six different tabs, the first one being the equivalent of a website's Homepage. On this page, there is a column where you can add your other YouTube accounts (a lot of YouTubers have a second account, with videos that don't fit in with the style of their main channel), as well as a list of related channels, i.e., a constant promo of other creators of your choice: maybe friends of yours who are also on YouTube or people you have met through the platform who you regularly collab with.

When you go to edit the main part of this page, you will see a drop-down list of content you can add to it, from which you can choose as many as you want. You can also choose how you want this content to be displayed: horizontally or vertically. So, on your profile homepage you can have:

Videos

- Your most popular videos, that is, the ones with the most views. They will be ordered from most viewed to least viewed.

- Your uploads, that will show up in order of upload date.

- Videos from other creators which you have "liked."

- Your posted videos.

- A live stream happening in that

moment.

- Your next live streams, so people know when to go on your profile and watch them.

- Your previous live streams, for people who did not have the chance to watch them in real time.

Playlists

- Playlists you have previously created.

- A unique playlist, which can be a list that someone else created on their profile, so long as you have the URL to that playlist.

- Saved playlists. The options that will show up for this one are all the lists from other creators you have ever saved while logged in to your account.

- Several playlists, that you can create on the spot.

- Published playlists that you have posted before.

Channels

- YouTube channels that you are subscribed to.

- Personalized groups created by yourself with the creators you want.

Others

- Recent activity.

- Recent messages.

Videos

The second tab on your profile is called

"Videos" and it is simply a list of all the videos you have ever posted, ordered either by upload date or by how popular they have gotten.

Playlists

Next, you have the "Playlists" tab. Here you will have all the playlists you create.

Channels

The fourth tab is related to channels and it shows the channels you are subscribed to. Here you can also add a link to your secondary channels.

Community

The Community tab is a very recent

addition to YouTube - it was introduced in 2018 - and it works like a feed where you can make posts that are not videos. You can choose to post text, or to complement it with an image, a GIF or a link to a YouTube video (yours or not) or to an external website. These posts will show up in your subscribers homepage, in between video posts, and they can like and comment on them.

About

The last tab is the one where you can add all your info: the "About." You can add a description of your channel and let people know what type of content they can expect to see; your business email, for any potential sponsors or partners to get in touch with you (or your manager); your location; and any links you want, such as your website or your profiles on other social media platforms. When other people visit your "About" tab they will also see the date when you first joined YouTube and the total number of views on your channel (and they will also have the option to report your account, but if you do everything as you should this is something you will not have to worry about).

Posting a Video

The main type of content you will be posting on YouTube is video. To do so, you will need to click the little video camera icon on the upper right corner of the website, and then select the file you will upload, which can be multiple formats (.mov, .mp4 and .avi are just a few of them) and should be horizontally oriented, with a ratio of 16:9. The dimensions can vary and they will determine the quality of video that will be available for the viewers. People will only be able to watch your videos on the worst quality available (240p) if a video is 426 pixels by 240 pixels. If you want your videos to be available on standard quality (480p), your video should be 854 pixels by 480 pixels; and, if you want them to be available on the highest quality (2160p), post them as 3840 pixels by 2160 pixels.

Once your video is uploaded, you can add the basic information (name, description and tags), translations for subtitles if you want it to be viewed by people who speak a different language than the one used in the video, and advanced settings regarding:

- **Comments**: if you allow anyone to comment, if you want comments with inappropriate language to be automatically deleted, or if you want the comment section to be disabled.

- **License and property rights**: where you can choose between YouTube's standard license or Creative Commons license. The first one states that you own the video and you give YouTube the permission to have it on their platform and share it, while by opting for the second one you allow other creators to use any part of the video for their own content.

- **Distribution options**: if you allow other people to embed your video on their website, if you want the video to appear on your subscribers feed, and if you want people with the notifications on for your videos to receive a notification for that specific video.

- **Age restrictions**: in case your video is not appropriate for minors. When a video is age restricted it gets automatically demonetized.

- **Category**.

- **Language**.

- **Community contributions**: if you want viewers to be able to contribute to the translation of your titles, descriptions, and subtitles in their own languages.

- **Recording date**.

- **Content declaration**: which, according to YouTube's Ad Policy, you are obligated to check in case your video has any paid endorsements.

You will also have the chance to choose the video's thumbnail, which is the image people see when your video shows up on their feed. YouTube will suggest frames of your video but, if you verify the phone number associated with your account, you get to upload any customized thumbnail you want (must be 1280 pixels by 720 pixels).

Once you publish the video, people will be able to give it a thumbs up if they like it, a thumbs down if they don't, share to specific people on YouTube (suggestions based on the email addresses you have contacted through Gmail) and to other social media platforms. They will also be able to save the video (on one of their YouTube playlists) and to comment on it, as long as you don't have that option disabled.

Youtube Ads

Is there such a thing as a social media platform without paid posts? Just like on the other three social networks covered before, business and personal brands can invest to advertise on YouTube. There are six types of ads you can create there:

- **Non-skippable video ads**: these ads are between 15 and 20 seconds long and the viewer is forced to watch them, if they want to be able to watch the content they clicked on.

- **TrueView ads**: these ads are skippable after 5 seconds and you only have to pay if the viewer watches 30 seconds. Considering most people skip the ads as soon as they can (unless those first 5 seconds are exquisite), financially this is a safe bet for you. TrueView ads can be In-Stream - the ones that appear before, during or after a video - or Discovery - the ones that appear on YouTube's SERPs, on the Watch page, and on YouTube's homepage. TrueView ads are the most commonly used on YouTube.

- **Bumpers**: six second videos that are also non-skippable and also play before, during or after a video.

- **In-display ads**: when you open a YouTube video, there is a column of suggestions for the next video you should watch. On top of those suggestions, you might see a paid video - that is a Display ad. These videos should be 300 pixels by 250 pixels or 300 pixels by 60 pixels.

- **Overlay ads:** these are those

banners you often see on the bottom of the player when you open a video and you can make them disappear by clicking on the cross icon on the upper right corner. The dimensions for these banners should either be 468 pixels by 60 pixels, or 728 pixels by 90 pixels.

- **Sponsored cards:** this last type of YouTube ad consists of the small cards with a CTA that sometimes appear when you are watching a video, and then automatically disappear after a while (unless the viewer clicked the cross on the right upper corner before). The dimensions of these cards can vary.

To start advertising on YouTube:

1. Go on Google Adwords.

2. Start a new campaign.

3. Choose between the standard delivery method (that shows your ads in a way that allows your budget to be distributed evenly throughout the days) or the accelerated one (which shows your ads as quickly as possible, from the moment you activate it).

4. Choose your network settings.

5. Choose your advanced settings: the start and end date, the ad rotation and the frequency (how many times a day your ad should play).

Youtube Statistics 2018

- In 2018, YouTube was the second largest social media network (after Facebook) (Aslam, 2019).

- There is 1.9 billion users visiting YouTube each month (Aslam, 2019).

- Every minute, 300 hours of content are uploaded to YouTube by 50 million creators (Aslam, 2019).

- There are 5 billion videos being watched every day (Aslam, 2019). In other words, 150 million hours (Aslam, 2019).

- There are 76 languages available on YouTube (Aslam, 2019).

- Users spend an average of 8 minutes and 41 seconds on YouTube every day (Cooper, 2019).

- 70% of YouTube's views are on mobile devices (Cooper, 2019).

- Compared to 2016, there are double the small and medium sized businesses advertising on YouTube (Cooper, 2019).

Personal Branding on Youtube in 2019

With video being such an effective type of content, there is space for everyone on YouTube. That becomes clear when we see how many people post on it. We see some creators become rich and famous thanks to YouTube and that makes us want to try.

But, because there are so many people on it, it is easy to get lost in the middle of so much content. So how can you stand out from all the other YouTubers?

Create good thumbnails

Thumbnails are the images that show up for your video when it is not playing (on YouTube's homepage or social media snippets when it is shared, for instance). They constitute a big part of why the user decides to watch your video or not, so you should definitely think them through in order to get as many views as possible.

Get a general template for your thumbnails so that it is easier for you to build them, and so that your profile does not look like a mess when someone visits your "Videos" tab. When it is time to make one for a specific video, try to use visuals and text that would make you get really curious and click. A good way of doing this is by using clickbait, that is, an over exaggeration of the content of the video (a couple of popular ones are "You won't believe what happened!" and "She/He said what?!"). Don't get too crazy with it though, otherwise people will just see you as someone who would say any lie just to get views. If you attract people and make them click play, you need to deliver great content.

Keep your video lists organized

If you have all your videos organized in lists, according to the topic you are covering or what type of content it is, the viewer will get to your profile and, first of all, get a clear idea of what he or she can expect to see from you; and secondly, if they have any specific topic in mind that they want to know more about, it will be way easier for them to find it. Remember that people don't want to have to spend a lot of time looking for the content they want, so if you have it easily available, the chances of you getting more views increases.

Use the Community tab

On YouTube, the big networking component of personal branding is a little bit harder to do than on other platforms. However, the Community tab was created to fill that void and it is definitely something to look at. So take full advantage of it: create text posts if you need to clarify anything, answer questions or just want to share some news; polls if you want to ask something to your subscribers, like what kind of content they would like to see from you in the future; images if you want to show new products or a sneak peek of future content; and GIFs to show your feelings and make your profile more fun and appealing. Make it worth it!

For Inspiration: a Youtube Branding Success

Liza Koshy did not start her online career on YouTube, but she is now one of the biggest content creators on the video platform and is slowly but surely making the transition from internet celebrity to "real" celebrity.

She currently has over 16 million subscribers on her main channel and over 7 million on her second channel. You see throughout her time on YouTube how much her content quality has evolved, from her 12 minute video introducing herself in 2015 to her show on YouTube Premium, Liza on Demand. However, something that did not ever change was her personality and that (along with creative, fun and well-edited content) is probably the biggest secret to her huge success.

She uses appealing thumbnails combined with clickbait, which makes everyone want to click and watch. She has good imagery, a complete bio and she updates her Community tab, making sure to use photos and GIFs to make the posts more engaging. She has won a number of awards, is now an actress and a TV host, and has a net worth of 4 million dollars, so... it works!

Chapter 11: Social Media Strategy Worksheet

Who do I want to talk to? Who is my target audience?

Which social media platforms am I going to use?

☐ Instagram

☐ Facebook

☐ Twitter

☐ YouTube

What are my goals for each of them?

Platform	Goals	

Am I going to invest in ads?

Platform	Type of ad	Budget	Goals
Facebook			
Instagram			

Which thought leaders should I follow?

Am I going to use any tools to aid me on the management of my pages?

What are my KPIs for each platform?

Chapter 12: Search Engine Optimization (SEO)

SEO (which stands for Search Engine Optimization) is an essential part of any brand that wants to grow their online presence, be it a personal brand or a business one, simply because we *all* use search engines (93% of website traffic is due to the use of search engines), but none of us really ever go on the second page of SERPs (75% of users never actually do it), unless it is an absolute necessity. This means that you should do everything in your power to be on the first page of results, ideally on the top of the list, so the user does not even have to scroll down to find you.

SEO Statistics 2018

- SEO has a conversion rate of 14,6% (Nikolovska, 2019).

- One search session typically lasts less than one minute (Jian, 2018). Understand why you need to be as high up on the list of results as possible?

- 43% of people state that they will do research on their phones even when they are already at the store, (almost) ready to buy something (Nikolovska, 2019).

- There are more than 73 000 searches happening on Google in just one second (1 Second - Internet Live Stats, n.d.).

- 81% of people do some research and read reviews before they spend money on something expensive

(Ahern, 2019).

- 70% of people pay way more attention to the organic search results than the paid ones, when they make an online research (Nikolovska, 2019).

SEO for Personal Branding

SEO can be on-page and off-page and, although a lot of people tend to focus on the first one, the off-page is probably the most important part. Here is what each of them encompasses. On-page SEO includes things that the user can see, such as the URL, the metadata and the images; while off-page SEO refers to what's behind the scenes of the website, like link building and guest blogging.

There is a specific type of SEO that can help you with your personal branding, conveniently called Personal SEO. It applies not only to your website, but also to your social media networks. In fact, I have already given you a few SEO suggestions in the chapters before, such as keeping the "About" tab on your profiles complete and using hashtags. But there is more to it than that.

Research the best keywords for your area of expertise

Google Adwords is a free, easy to understand tool that you can use to find the right words and expressions to use in your profiles and website in order to generate traffic. Ubersuggest, a tool created by Neil Patel (an entrepreneur and analytics expert, whose personal branding strategies are definitely also worth taking a look at) is also a really good option, which has been updated with new features recently, the newest one being the chance to have a better understanding of how your competitors are using their keywords and using that as inspiration, simply by typing the competitors domain on the tool.

On page 67 you will find a very simple SEO worksheet that you can use to make your keyword research. However, if it all seems to complicated or time-consuming, you can always leave this job to a professional, since it is quite an easy task to outsource.

Use them in every platform you are on

BUT keep in mind that optimizing your online presence with SEO is more (way more) than just adding a bunch of keywords to your website (or profile) or, in other words, doing keyword stuffing. In fact, if Google realizes you are doing that instead of using those words where it makes sense, your website's ranking can be negatively affected. This happens because Google's algorithms can assess when you are using keywords in places where it does not make sense, when you use too many of them, or if you are using transparent text to add even more keywords to the page.

Proofread your posts before you publish them to the world

You should always proofread simply because grammar and spelling mistakes are never a good look for anyone, no matter what industry they work in. But SEO is one more reason to add to that. Even if you do use the right keywords in the right places, if Google realizes that the readability of your website is not good, your ranking will be harmed. Grammar and spelling are two of the things that make a page readable or not, so always take a double (or triple) look at your content before it goes live.

If you want to go an extra step further, you can either invest on spelling online tools and apps or hire a freelance proofreader/editor to review your content. Two heads (or one head and one online tool) think better than one!

Find a way for your name to stand out, especially if it is a common one

If you have a really common name and surname, when a person googles it, you will be one of way too many and people don't have time, so they will probably not bother going through each person on the results page until they find you. You need to have a more unique name. Two ways you can do this are by adding your middle name to it (or even using just your second name plus your last name, if it makes a more unique combination) or creating an artistic name. Don't be afraid to do some trial and error until you find the name that works best for you.

Remember Liza Koshy, the YouTube star mentioned a couple of chapters ago? Her name is not actually Liza, it is Elizabeth. Now, the change was not crazy, but it was enough that when we are talking about YouTubers and someone mentions Liza, the YouTube community automatically knows it is her being referred to. She does not even need her last name anymore!

If your name is already unique, you are a lucky one. Go with it!

Adam Schaffner

Chapter 13: SEO Worksheet

Think of possible keywords that would work for your website. Remember these don't need to be one word only, they can be expressions. In fact, half of the search queries people use have four words or more.

Tip: if you can't think of many, use Google Suggests. So, if you were a Freelance Writer for example, you would type in "freelance writer" on Google's search bar and see the suggestions that would come up below.

Go on your tool of choice and start your keyword research and fill in the table with the data.

Topic	Keyword	Search Volume

How do your competitors perform when it comes to SEO?

With all of this in mind, choose the best keywords, that you will use on your website.

Chapter 14: Tips and Tricks to Social Media Marketing and SEO Success in 2019

When you create and manage your posts, ask yourself how do you want other people to see you. *But* stay true to who you are. Find a balance between those two and create the best version of yourself, that will make other people in your industry become curious as to who you are and how they can network with you.

Keep all your social media profiles (as well as your website) consistent. If a user goes on your Facebook and sees you as one type of person, and then goes on your Twitter profile, and sees someone completely different, that will just lead to confusion. It is okay to adapt to the different platforms, as long as you don't lose the essence of who you are in the process.

This consistency also applies to the visuals you use, which should have the same design basis all throughout your digital presence; and the usernames you go for, which, in a perfect world, would be the same on every platform. However, that is virtually impossible nowadays because so many people are online and so many user handles are already taken. Still, try your best to keep them similar.

Share your posts from one platform on other platforms. For example, whenever you post a video on YouTube, make a post about it on Twitter. That way, a Twitter follower of yours can also become a YouTube subscriber and your subscriber count goes up. Plus it is an easy way of continuously feeding your profiles.

Another good idea would be to include a feed of one of your profiles (the one you update more regularly would be the best choice) on your website. This is quite easy to do, since for every social platform and every Content Management System (CMS) you will find instructions on how to embed whichever feed you wish. For the other social platforms, make sure to have an icon linking to your profile. A lot of CMS show you that option when you are editing your website's footer, header, or menu. It should be easy to find, but in case you can't, it is nothing a simple Google research won't solve.

Never, ever forget mobile. With the continuous rise of smartphones and with no one being able to go one single day without data or access to Wi-Fi, not having the mobile world in mind when you work on your digital presence is a sin. So, optimize your website for mobile and make sure it is responsive (i.e., that its layout adapts to the dimensions of all devices, from the biggest computer screen to the smallest phone one). Besides that, use images with the dimensions that each platform suggests and don't include text with small fonts in them, otherwise people using their phones will not be able to properly read it. And one statistic, in case you need more convincing: in 2017, 67% of people who use their mobile phone to make online searches stated that they are more likely to make a purchase if their website is optimized for mobile (Clifford, 2017).

Engage, engage, engage. I have highlighted the importance of interacting with others so many times throughout this book and that is for a reason! There is no point in working to build the best personal brand in the entire world (wide web) if in the end you don't communicate with others and explore opportunities that might come up.

Invest in paid posts. Everybody is online, yet organic traffic is dead. The way around this problem: sponsored content. There is no need to spend a crazy amount of money or to sponsor every single post you make on every single platform, but thinking strategically and investing on certain posts can make your online following grow exponentially, so make sure to save a bit of your marketing budget to spend on social.

Make sure to include your name and job title in each platform. It does not have to be your name, as I have said before, but for SEO (and consistency) purposes, it is crucial that you introduce yourself the same way everywhere. For the job title, use your keyword research tool and find the more profitable version of it.

Keep an eye on your pages' KPIs. Every platform gives you information on how your posts are doing and through that, you can understand what works and what doesn't work for your (ideal) audience and then, make the necessary adjustments in order to keep growing.

Conclusion

Creating and nourishing your personal brand is hard work and in the beginning you might even feel a bit overwhelmed, but it is definitely a big step towards your success and once you get a hang of it, you will see how worth it it is. Nowadays, I would dare to say there is not one recruiter or potential partner who does not look up their candidates online, so taking some time (and some money) to make sure that when they do, they will be nothing but pleased and excited to work with you, can lead you to great achievements.

Thank you for reading this book, I hope it inspired you to work on your personal brand and helped you figure out which steps you should take. Good luck!

References

Searchengineland.com. (n.d.). What is SEO / Search Engine Optimization? - Search Engine Land. Retrieved from: https://searchengineland.com/guide/what -is-seo [Accessed 24 Mar. 2019].

Eisenberg, H. (2014). Humans Process Visual Data Better. Retrieved from: http://www.t-sciences.com/news/humans-process-visual-data-better [Accessed 24 Mar. 2019].

Chaffey, D. (2019). Global social media research summary 2019 | Smart Insights. Retrieved from: https://www.smartinsights.com/social-media-marketing/social-media-strategy/new-global-social-media-research/ [Accessed 24 Mar. 2019].

Kemp, S. (2018). Digital in 2018: World's internet users pass the 4 billion mark - We

Are Social UK - Global Socially-Led Creative Agency. Retrieved from: https://wearesocial.com/uk/blog/2018/01 /global-digital-report-2018 [Accessed 24 Mar. 2019].

Estrada, M. (2017). 5 Reasons Why Personal Branding is Important. Retrieved from: https://www.careermetis.com/reasons-personal-branding-is-important/ [Accessed 24 Mar. 2019].

Basu, T. (n.d.). How to Build a Personal Brand (Complete Guide to Personal Branding. Retrieved from: https://www.thinkific.com/blog/personal-branding-guide/ [Accessed 24 Mar. 2019].

Bangera, J. (2018). 6 Amazing Benefits of Personal Branding. Retrieved from: https://blog.inkjetwholesale.com.au/mark eting-advertising/6-amazing-benefits-personal-branding/ [Accessed 24 Mar. 2019].

Blog.kajabi.com. (2018). What is Personal Branding, Why It's Important, Benefits & Examples. Retrieved from: https://blog.kajabi.com/what-is-personal-branding-why-it-s-important-benefits-examples [Accessed 24 Mar. 2019].

Newoldstamp.com. (n.d.). Be an Expert: 10 Tips to Create an Awesome Personal Brand - NEWOLDSTAMP. Retrieved from: https://newoldstamp.com/blog/be-an-expert-10-tips-to-create-an-awesome-personal-brand/ [Accessed 25 Mar. 2019].

Forbes.com. (2018). Council Post: 10 Tips For Developing A Strong Personal Brand. Retrieved from: https://www.forbes.com/sites/forbesagencycouncil/2018/07/21/10-tips-for-developing-a-strong-personal-brand/#725d4c71b705 [Accessed 25 Mar. 2019].

Forbes.com. (2018). 3 Simples Steps To Build Your Personal Brand. Retrieved from: https://www.forbes.com/sites/womensmedia/2018/09/06/3-simple-steps-to-build-your-personal-brand/#7f5073a63776 [Accessed 25 Mar. 2019].

Forbes.com. (2018). Council Post: Branding Yourself? Follow These 14 Tips To Build Your Strategy. Retrieved from: https://www.forbes.com/sites/forbescoachescouncil/2018/04/18/branding-yourself-follow-these-14-tips-to-build-your-strategy/#1e5609bf29ec [Accessed 25 Mar. 2019].

Brandyourcareer.com. (n.d.). Personal Branding Workbook. [PDF] Available at: http://www.brandyourcareer.com/docs/Pe

rsonal%20_Branding_Workbook.pdf
[Accessed 25 Mar. 2019].

Pwc.com. (n.d.).
personal_brand_workbook.pdf. [PDF]
Available at:
https://www.pwc.com/c1/en/assets/downl
oads/personal_brand_workbook.pdf
[Accessed 25 Mar. 2019].

Instazood.com. (2018). The History of
Instagram | Instazood. Retrieved from:
https://instazood.com/the-history-of-
instagram/ [Accessed 25 Mar. 2019].

Moreau, E. (2019). What Is Instagram and
Why Should You Be Using It? Retrieved
from: https://www.lifewire.com/what-is-
instagram-3486316 [Accessed 25 Mar.
2019].

Help.instagram.com. (n.d.). How are
photos and videos chosen for Search &
Explore? | Instagram Help Center.

Retrieved   from:
https://help.instagram.com/48722456129
6752 [Accessed 25 Mar. 2019].

Meetedgar.com.   (2018).   Instagram
Business Account or Personal Account -
What's   the   Difference?   -   MeedEdgar.
[online]   Available   at.
https://meetedgar.com/blog/instagram-
business-account-whats-the-difference/
[Accessed 25 Mar. 2019].

Chacon, B. (2017). Should You Switch to an
Instagram   Business   Profile?
{INFOGRAPHIC}   Retrieved   from:
https://later.com/blog/instagram-
business-profile/ [Accessed 25 Mar. 2019]

Campbell, C. (2019). Instagram Ads: How
to   Advertise   on   Instagram   in   2019.
Retrieved   from:
https://www.shopify.com/blog/instagram-
ads#types [Accessed 25 Mar. 2019].

Aslam, S. (2019). Instagram by the Numbers (2019): Stats, Demographics & Fun Facts. Retrieved from: https://www.omnicoreagency.com/instagram-statistics/ [Accessed 26 Mar. 2019].

Agrawal, S. (2019). Instagram Statistics 2019: Know The Latest Instagram By The Numbers. Retrieved from: https://www.digitalgyd.com/instagram-statistics/#instagram-demographics [Accessed 26 Mar. 2019].

McLaren, L. (2018). Top 35 Instagram Statistics of 2018. Retrieved from: https://www.esocmedia.com/instagram-marketing/top-35-instagram-statistics-of-2018/ [Accessed 26 Mar. 2019].

Clarke, T. (2019). 22+ Instagram Statistics That Matter to Marketers in 2019. Retrieved from: https://blog.hootsuite.com/instagram-statistics/ [Accessed 26 Mar. 2019].

Forsey, C. (2018). The Ultimate Guide to Instagram Hashtags for 2019. Retrieved from:

https://blog.hubspot.com/marketing/instagram-hashtags [Accessed 26 Mar. 2019].

Kalish, A. (n.d.). How Do I Brand Myself on Instagram? - The Muse. Retrieved from:

https://www.themuse.com/advice/guide-personal-brand-instagram [Accessed 26 Mar. 2019].

Crazyegg.com. (2016). The Exact Formula For Growing Your Personal Brand on Instagram (With Examples). Retrieved from:

https://www.crazyegg.com/blog/growing-your-personal-brand-on-instagram/ [Accessed 26 Mar. 2019].

Donelly, G. (2019). Everything You Need to Know About Instagram Story Ads |

Wordstream. Retrieved from: https://www.wordstream.com/blog/ws/20 18/08/07/instagram-story-ads [Accessed 26 Mar. 2019].

Carbone, L. (2018). Instagram Stories Analytics: Every Metric You Need to Know. Retrieved from: https://later.com/blog/instagram-stories-analytics/ [Accessed 26 Mar. 2019].

Fleck, A. (2018). 8 Influencers Share 8 Ways to Make Your Instagram Story More Engaging. Retrieved from: https://www.adweek.com/digital/8-influencers-share-8-ways-to-make-your-instagram-story-more-engaging/ [Accessed 26 Mar. 2019].

Ellis, K. (2018, Sept 5). Facebook Ads vs. Boosted Posts: What is the Difference?. Retrieved from: https://zestsms.com/about/blog/facebook

-ads-vs-boosted-posts-what-is-the-difference/ [Accessed 28 Mar. 2019].

Facebook.com. (2019, Mar 7). The Difference Between Boosted Posts and Facebook Ads. Retrieved from: https://www.facebook.com/business/help /317083072148603 [Accessed 27 Mar. 2019].

Fairbrother, P. (2019, Jan 7). How To Master Facebook Business Manager (the 2019 Guide). Retrieved from: https://adespresso.com/blog/facebook-business-manager-guide/ [Accessed 28 Mar. 2019].

Facebook.com. (n.d.). Facebook ad formats for different goals | Facebook Business. Retrieved from: https://www.facebook.com/business/ads/ ad-formats?ref=ads_guide [Accessed 28 Mar. 2019].

Facebook.com. (n.d.). Advertising with stories ads: Fast and immersive full-screen format | Facebook Business. Retrieved from: https://www.facebook.com/business/ads/stories-ad-format [Accessed 29 Mar. 2019].

Clifford, R. (2017, Sep 28). 5 Reasons Your Website should be Mobile Friendly | Inkwell Creative Media. Retrieved from: https://www.inkwellcreativemedia.com/5-reasons-your-website-should-be-mobile-friendly/ [Accessed 3 April 2019].

Facebook.com. (n.d.). Facebook Messenger ads: Your ads on Messenger | Facebook Business. Retrieved from: https://www.facebook.com/business/ads/messenger-ads [Accessed 3 April 2019].

Facebook.com. (n.d.). Facebook carousel format: multiple images and text in one ad | Facebook Business. Retrieved from:

https://www.facebook.com/business/ads/ carousel-ad-format [Accessed 3 April 2019].

Facebook.com. (n.d.). How Facebook slideshow ads work | Facebook Business. Retrieved from: https://www.facebook.com/business/ads/ slideshow-ad-format [Accessed 3 April 2019].

Facebook.com. (n.d.). Facebook collection ad format | Facebook Business. Retrieved from: https://www.facebook.com/business/ads/ collection-ad-format# [Accessed 3 April 2019].

Facebook.com. (n.d.). Facebook playable ad formats: Create interactive app previews | Facebook Business. Retrieved from: https://www.facebook.com/business/ads/ playable-ad-format [Accessed 3 April

2019].

Facebook.com. (n.d.). How video ads work on Facebook | Facebook Business. Retrieved from: https://www.facebook.com/business/ads/video-ad-format [Accessed 3 April 2019].

Facebook.com. (n.d.). Advertising with stories ads: Fast and immersive full-screen format | Facebook Business. Retrieved from: https://www.facebook.com/business/ads/stories-ad-format [Accessed 3 April 2019].

Duron, M. (2014, Jan 16). Can Personal Brands Use Facebook Ads? - Personal Branding Blog - Stand Out In Your Career. Retrieved from: http://www.personalbrandingblog.com/can-personal-brands-use-facebook-ads/ [Accessed 3 April 2019].

Outbrain.com (n.d.). What Is Native

Advertising- How it works? | Outbrain.com. Retrieved from: https://www.outbrain.com/native-advertising/ [Accessed 3 April 2019].

Myers, L. (2019, Jan 11). Social Media Cheat Sheet 2019: Must-Have Image Sizes! Retrieved from: https://louisem.com/2852/social-media-cheat-sheet-sizes#twitter [Accessed 3 April 2019].

Pinegar, G. (2018, July 19). What is Twitter: A Beginner's Guide. Retrieved from: https://learn.g2crowd.com/what-is-twitter [Accessed 3 April 2019].

Developer.twitter.com (n.d.). Summary Card - Twitter Developers. Retrieved from: https://developer.twitter.com/en/docs/tweets/optimize-with-cards/overview/summary [Accessed 3 April 2019].

Developer.twitter.com (n.d.). Summary with large image - Twitter Developers. Retrieved from: https://developer.twitter.com/en/docs/tweets/optimize-with-cards/overview/summary-card-with-large-image.html [Accessed 3 April 2019].

Developer.twitter.com (n.d.). App card - Twitter Developers. Retrieved from: https://developer.twitter.com/en/docs/tweets/optimize-with-cards/overview/app-card [Accessed 3 April 2019].

Carter, R. (2018, Dec. 2018). Twitter Cards: Everything you need to know | Sprout Social. Retrieved from: https://sproutsocial.com/insights/twitter-cards-guide/ [Accessed 3 April 2019].

Help.twitter.com. (n.d.). How to use hashtags. Retrieved from: https://help.twitter.com/en/using-twitter/how-to-use-hashtags [Accessed 3 April 2019].

Lee, K. (2014, Oct 15). How to Use Twitter Analytics: The Complete Guide. Retrieved from: https://help.twitter.com/en/using-twitter/how-to-use-hashtags [Accessed 3 April 2019].

Zephoria.com (2019). Top 10 Twitter Statistics - Updated March 2019 - Zephoria Digital Marketing. Retrieved from: https://zephoria.com/twitter-statistics-top-ten/ [Accessed 3 April 2019].

Cooper, P. (2019, Jan 16). 28 Twitter Statistics All Marketers Need to Know in 2019. Retrieved from: https://blog.hootsuite.com/twitter-statistics/ [Accessed 3 April 2019].

Help.twitter.com. (n.d.). About public and protected Tweets. Retrieved from: https://help.twitter.com/en/safety-and-

security/public-and-protected-tweets
[Accessed 3 April 2019].

Sabanty, C. (2019, Jan 11). The Top 58 Most Popular Hashtags to Get Likes and Retweets on Twitter. Retrieved from: https://blog.hubspot.com/marketing/best-hashtags-twitter [Accessed 3 April 2019].

Patel, N. (2015, April 17). How To Grow Your PErsonal Brand On Twitter In Only 10 Minutes A Day - Marketing Land. Retrieved from: https://marketingland.com/how-to-grow-your-personal-brand-on-twitter-in-only-10-minutes-a-day-121514 [Accessed 3 April 2019].

McCorkle, D. (2014, Oct 2). Do's and Don'ts: Using Twitter for Personal Branding and Job Search | Social Media Today. Retrieved from: https://www.socialmediatoday.com/conte

nt/dos-and-donts-using-twitter-personal-branding-and-job-search [Accessed 3 April 2019].

Lua, A. (2018, Oct 4). Retweeting Your Own Tweets Cards Can Boost Your Reach and Engagement. Retrieved from: https://buffer.com/resources/twitter-retweet-experiment [Accessed 3 April 2019].

Kay, D. (2018, May 1). How To Automatically Retweet your Own Tweets for 3-4X Engagement | Deborah Kay. Retrieved from: https://www.digitaldiscovery.sg/blog/how-to-automatically-retweet-your-own-tweets/ [Accessed 3 April 2019].

Francisti, A. (2018, Sep 5). The Ultimate Guide to YouTube Banner Size and Design - LeadQuizzes Blog. Retrieved from: https://blog.leadquizzes.com/the-ultimate-guide-to-youtube-banner-size-and-design/ [Accessed 3 April 2019].

LoDolce, A. (2018). Set up a YouTube Channel: Yout Step-By-Step Guide - Viewership Media. Retrieved from: https://viewership.com/setup-youtube-channel-guide-2018/ [Accessed 3 April 2019].

McCabe, K. (2018, Dec 21). The Perfect YouTube Video Size for 2019: Dimensions, Resolution, and Aspect Ratio. Retrieved from: https://learn.g2crowd.com/youtube-video-size [Accessed 3 April 2019].

Youtube.com (n.d.). YouTube Advertising - Online Video Advertising Campaigns. Retrieved from: https://www.youtube.com/yt/advertise/ [Accessed 3 April 2019].

Cooper, P. (2019, Jan 22). 22 YouTube Stats That Matter to Marketers in 2019.

Retrieved from: https://blog.hootsuite.com/youtube-stats-marketers/ [Accessed 3 April 2019].

Aslam, S. (2019, Jan 6). YouTube by the Numbers (2019): Stats, Demographics & Fun Facts. Retrieved from: https://www.omnicoreagency.com/youtube-statistics/ [Accessed 3 April 2019].

Brown, C. (2017, Oct 4). Why YouTube Thumbnails Matter - Octoly Magazine. Retrieved from: https://mag.octoly.com/youtube-thumbnails-matter-563c9af6fa74 [Accessed 3 April 2019].

Western, D. (n.d.). Liza Koshy's Net Worth in 2019 | Wealthy Gorilla. Retrieved from: https://wealthygorilla.com/liza-koshy-net-worth/ [Accessed 3 April 2019].

Joyce, S. (n.d.). Guide to Personal SEO for Job Search and Careers - Job-Hunt.org.

Retrieved from: https://www.job-hunt.org/personal-SEO/personal-SEO.shtml [Accessed 3 April 2019].

Blue, S. (2012, Jan 22). Personal Branding: 3 tips for personal SEO | MarketingSherpa Blog. Retrieved from: https://sherpablog.marketingsherpa.com/marketing-careers/personal-seo-tips/ [Accessed 3 April 2019].

Nikolovska, H. (2019, Feb 5). 60+ SEO Statistics to Help You Rank #1 in 2019 - SEO Tribunal. Retrieved from: https://seotribunal.com/blog/stats-to-understand-seo/#general-seo-statistics-2019 [Accessed 3 April 2019].

Exabytes.com (2018, Nov 15). [Infographic] 10 Must-Know SEO Statistics for 2018 - Exabytes.com. Retrieved from: https://www.exabytes.com/blog/10-must-know-seo-statistics-for-2018/ [Accessed 3

April 2019].

Ahern, P. (2019, Feb 26). 25 Mind-Bottling SEO Stats for 2019 & Beyond | SEO Insights | Junto. Retrieved from: https://junto.digital/blog/seo-stats/ [Accessed 3 April 2019].

Kimgarst.com (n.d). A Step-by-Step Guide to SEO Keyword Research Using FREE Tools. Retrieved from: https://kimgarst.com/stepbystep-guide-seo-keyword-research-free-tools/ [Accessed 3 April 2019].

Neilpatel.com. (n.d.). Ubersuggest's Free Keyword Tool, Generate More Suggestions. Retrieved from: https://neilpatel.com/ubersuggest/ [Accessed 3 April 2019].

Dalley, S. (2016, Sep 13). Why proofreading is important for SEO | GrowTraffic™. Retrieved from: https://www.growtraffic.co.uk/why-

proofreading-is-important-for-seo/
[Accessed 3 April 2019].

Rao, K. (2018, Sep 3). 6 Types of Ads you can display on Youtube and How to advertise on Youtube? - Whizsky. Retrieved from:
https://www.whizsky.com/2018/09/6-types-of-ads-you-can-display-on-youtube/
[Accessed 3 April 2019].

Chacon, B. (2018, Oct 13). Instagram Image Size & Dimensions for 2018 (+ Free Infographic!) - Later Blog. Retrieved from:
https://later.com/blog/instagram-image-size/ [Accessed 3 April 2019].

Moz.com. (n.d.). Off-Page SEO | Learn SEO - Moz. Retrieved from:
https://moz.com/learn/seo/off-site-seo
[Accessed 3 April 2019].

Made in the USA
Monee, IL
01 November 2019

16183774R00118